IN THE

NATIONAL INTEREST

General Sir John Monash once exhorted a graduating class to 'equip yourself for life, not solely for your own benefit but for the benefit of the whole community'. At the university established in his name, we repeat this statement to our own graduating classes, to acknowledge how important it is that common or public good flows from education.

Universities spread and build on the knowledge they acquire through scholarship in many ways, well beyond the transmission of this learning through education. It is a necessary part of a university's role to debate its findings, not only with other researchers and scholars, but also with the broader community in which it resides.

Publishing for the benefit of society is an important part of a university's commitment to free intellectual inquiry. A university provides civil space for such inquiry by its scholars, as well as for investigations by public intellectuals and expert practitioners.

This series, In the National Interest, embodies Monash University's mission to extend knowledge and encourage informed debate about matters of great significance to Australia's future.

Professor Sharon Pickering
President and Vice-Chancellor,
Monash University

KATE FITZ-GIBBON

OUR NATIONAL CRISIS: VIOLENCE AGAINST WOMEN & CHILDREN

Monash University Publishing
Matheson Library Annexe
40 Exhibition Walk
Monash University
Clayton, Victoria 3800, Australia
https://publishing.monash.edu

Monash University Publishing brings to the world publications which advance the best traditions of humane and enlightened thought.

ISBN: 9781922979933 (paperback)
ISBN: 9781922979957 (ebook)

Series: In the National Interest
Editor: Greg Bain
Project manager & copyeditor: Paul Smitz
Designer: Peter Long
Typesetter: Cannon Typesetting
Proofreader: Gillian Armitage
Printed in Australia by Ligare Book Printers

A catalogue record for this book is available from the National Library of Australia.

The paper this book is printed on is in accordance with the standards of the Forest Stewardship Council®. The FSC® promotes environmentally responsible, socially beneficial and economically viable management of the world's forests.

For my trio—Matilda, William and Edward. You are my driving motivation to end violence against women and children. I believe in a safer future for you and for all Australian children and young people.

For Michael—I am so thankful for a partner who champions me, encourages me to dream, and supports me in making those dreams come true. Thank you.

OUR NATIONAL CRISIS: VIOLENCE AGAINST WOMEN & CHILDREN

For over a decade, I have studied the killing of women by men's violence. From my own work, and a global body of research from which I draw, I know that this violence is inherently preventable, and within that knowledge lies hope—the hope that improved responses, more effective early interventions and a true commitment to prevention, all spearheaded by sustained national leadership, *will* drive down the rates of women killed by men known to them.

Over the last six months, however, more often than not that sense of hope has turned into anger and despair. My newly minted academic self in 2012 thought we would be further ahead by now. As recently as three years ago, when my book *Our National Shame* was published, I felt that the catalyst for change might be at hand. But I appreciate now perhaps better than ever how significant the challenge is, how profound the crisis of men's violence against women and children in Australia is.

In 2024, over twelve years after I completed my PhD examining the sentencing of men who killed their female intimate partners in Australia, I have been reminded all too often of the pertinence of a quote from author Margaret Atwood: 'Men are afraid that women will laugh at them. Women are afraid that men will kill them.' While the quote is around forty years old, it remains starkly relevant. The horrific events of 2024 in Australia demonstrate that women continue to have good reason to fear men's violence.

In mid-February, emergency services attended a rural property in Queensland where they found 41-year-old Amarjit Kaur Sardar, who had died from injuries sustained from being run over by the slasher attachment on a tractor. Amarjit's husband was charged with her murder. He reported that his wife died as the result of an accident.[1]

Just three weeks later, in early March, the body of Chaithanya 'Swetha' Madhagani was discovered by police in a green waste bin on an isolated road in Victoria. It is alleged that her husband, who in the period between Swetha's death and the discovery of her body had flown to India with their son, confessed to her killing.[2] However, no arrest has been made over Swetha's killing, and the investigations continue.

In early April 2024, the body of 21-year-old Hannah McGuire was found in a burnt-out wreck of a car in regional Victoria. Hannah's former partner, a 21-year-old male, was charged shortly afterwards with her murder. The mayor of the local council, Brian Hood, said, 'I think for most of us it is pretty difficult to comprehend how and why these sorts of events happen.'[3]

A few weeks later, in late April, the body of thirty-year-old Erica Hay was found by emergency services personnel attending a house fire in a southern suburb of Perth. It is alleged that Erica's partner set the fire after assaulting her, before fleeing the house with her three-year-old child.[4] Erica's partner has been charged with her murder.

It will take time for the full circumstances of each of these cases to come to light as they progress through the justice process. While in several cases arrests have been made, it is important to note that those charges have not yet been through the court process, and I absolutely recognise the importance of the presumption of innocence until proven guilty. What is not in question is that each of these women are dead, their lives taken.

There are many more deaths I could describe here, but I hope I've made my point with these shocking stories. In each one, a woman is killed, their bodies disposed of in a bin, in a car, on a deserted property, in their own home where they had every right to feel safe. It's a truism to say that women's lives matter, but then why is it that in 2024, the intensity of fatal attacks on women has reached a level not seen for over a decade in Australia?

The women listed here represent only a small number of the women killed in Australia in 2024 alone. According to Counting Death Women Australia, a voluntary initiative led by researchers from the online group Destroy the Joint, in the first six months of this year, at least thirty-nine women have been killed by men's violence. In recent years, on average, at least one woman has been killed each week by men's violence in Australia—in 2022 this equated to the deaths of fifty-seven women nationally; in 2023, at least sixty-four women were killed.

There have also been times in recent years when the frequency with which women have been killed has raised greater alarm among policymakers and advocates. In late October and early November 2023, over a ten-day period, a woman was killed in Australia every two days. Each of the five killings occurred in a different Australian state or territory and involved a range of different circumstances, but they all had two things in common: the alleged use of fatal male violence, and that the alleged male perpetrators were known to the female victim prior to her death. Writing in *The Canberra Times* at the time, Griffith University Professor Silke Meyer and I exclaimed that, 'While these recent deaths have been largely met with silence from those in leadership, domestic and family violence advocates and practitioners are screaming from the trenches.'[5]

There are echoes here of late 2018, when six Australian women were killed by men's violence over a five-day period. The deaths of these women elicited little outcry and even less political acknowledgement or calls for action. As I wrote in *Our National Shame*, Australian journalist Jane Gilmour said this about the relative silence: 'Our compassion is fatigued by the daily drain of women being beaten, raped, assaulted, ignored, dismissed, blamed, ridiculed, murdered. How exhausted we all are by the violence women live and die with'.[6] Within a week of the Gilmour article, two more women had been killed in Australia.

Further cementing awareness of the depth of the crisis we face, throughout 2024 there have been numerous instances of children in Australia killed, most often—but not exclusively—allegedly by adult men known to them. This includes two-year-old Rowan Roome, a ten-year-old girl, a sixteen-year-old boy and a seven-year-old boy, all in New South Wales, and a one-year-old boy in Victoria.[7] As I was finalising this book, news reports rolled in of three children allegedly killed by their father in a house fire in Lalor Park, New South Wales. Speaking shortly following the killings, the state premier described the killings as leaving 'a deep wound on the state'.[8]

I have deliberately chosen to begin this book with these awful stories. I worry that as a community, we are becoming—or have become—desensitised to women's deaths. And what of the international context? How to communicate what the global toll of men's violence against women and children means in terms of our day-to-day lives? Consider that the 'average' Australian reads between 200 and 300 words per minute. By this measure, it will take an average Australian anywhere between sixty and ninety minutes to read this book. The brutal reality is that in that time, it is estimated that at least five women—and potentially up to eight women—around the world will die from men's violence. On average, a woman is killed once every eleven minutes.[9]

This is a distressing reality, but one that we must acknowledge. It is only through acknowledgement, by shining a fierce light on the problem, that we can drive the transformational change so desperately needed.

THE TIP OF THE ICEBERG

The women killed by men's violence represent only the tip of the iceberg when it comes to the problem of male violence. When we focus only on deaths, we risk ignoring the full extent of what lurks beneath the fatalities.

The prevalence of domestic, family and sexual violence is difficult to quantify given that acts of violence against women so often go unreported to the police. It is estimated that almost nine in ten incidents of sexual assault are not reported. When asked why they did not alert the police to such abuse, just over a third of the women respondents said they believed they could deal with the incident themselves, while another third said they did not regard the incident as a serious offence. Even more concerning, a quarter of the women cited feelings of shame or embarrassment as factors contributing to their unwillingness to go to the police.[10] It is a dire reflection of contemporary community attitudes that the majority of women in Australia who experience sexual violence carry the burden of shame for the sexually violent actions of men.

The barriers to reporting sexual violence are also experienced by victims of other forms of gender-based violence. Almost half of the women who experience violence from a current or former intimate partner do not seek any advice or support, and over 80 per cent never contact the police to report that violence.[11] These statistics are even more alarming when you consider that, Australia-wide, it has been estimated that on average, police respond to a domestic and family violence incident every two minutes.[12] In far too many instances, that call is never made.

During countless research interviews with victim-survivors of intimate partner violence over the years, I have listened to individuals recount the reasons why they did not report their victimisation to police. I have come to understand the challenges faced by victim-survivors, many of whom hold a deep distrust of the police and the justice system, and some of whom, by virtue of the abuse they have experienced, have lost the sense of independence and confidence within themselves to disclose their abuse to a support service or justice agency.

During an interview I conducted in 2021 with Ash (a pseudonym used in order to protect her identity), a woman in her forties living in Western Australia, I asked her why she had not told anyone about her experience of coercive control, a pattern of abusive behaviours I will explore in more detail shortly. Ash explained:

> I didn't have the words to say what was happening to me. I didn't know what it was. I had this feeling, always feeling sick, nervous, anxious, stressed. I knew something wasn't right but I didn't know what it was, didn't know what to say but didn't know who to ask for help. And it's also the shame. How could I let this happen? How come [when] I'm a strong, intelligent person with a good job and a degree? How did I get fooled by this person?
>
> And there's also the fact that … they're charismatic and they're charming. And every time they think they're about to lose you, they draw [you] back in. And they're so good at that and you think, no, they're that person. What I've since learnt is, no, the true person they are is actually that bad side. And all the rest is actually the window-dressing, to keep you toeing the line.

Given the low level of reporting to justice agencies, the most reliable prevalence estimates we have in Australia, beyond criminal justice system data, come from the Australian Bureau of Statistics Personal Safety Survey. The survey collects data on self-reported rates of victimisation among Australians since the age of fifteen, and over the past twelve months. According to the latest findings, released in 2023, eight million Australians have experienced violence since the age of fifteen.[13] This means that:

- one in four women, and one in fourteen men, have experienced intimate partner violence
- one in five women, and one in sixteen men, have experienced sexual violence
- one in three women, and two in five men, have experienced physical violence
- one in five women, and one in fifteen men, have experienced stalking.

In many instances, these different forms of violence will not be perpetrated in isolation from one another. Some victim-survivors experience multiple forms of abuse during an abusive relationship, and in some cases in numerous abusive relationships throughout their lives.

While men's violence against women can take many different forms—be it physical, sexualised, intimidatory, or focused on property or pets, for example—all of these are underpinned and linked by the male desire for power and control over women. When the motivation for violence is viewed from this perspective, it is not surprising to learn that the breakdown of a relationship and the period of separation immediately after can be a time of incredible risk for women and children. It is when women attempt to assert their independence, when they attempt to live an individual life, when *his* control over her is at threat, that they are at the greatest risk of serious—all too often fatal—violence.

In a reflection of the evolving understanding of different forms of abuse, the most recent Personal Safety Survey was the first to collect data on economic abuse among co-habiting partners. Economic abuse was defined as behaviours or actions 'aimed at preventing or controlling a person's access to economic resources, causing them emotional harm or fear'.[14] The survey shows that one in six women, and one in thirteen men, have experienced this type of abuse since the age of fifteen.

Economic abuse can involve a wide range of abusive behaviours. Guidance provided to members of the Australian judiciary details numerous scenarios of economic and financial abuse, including

> controlling the victim's access to finances and income. For example, victims may be refused access to, or information about, bank accounts … Sometimes

> perpetrators may exploit the victim's finances or coerce the victim to take on debt. Examples include perpetrators taking out credit cards in the victim's name without the victim's knowledge, coercing the victim to sign a contract for the provision of finance, a loan or credit, coercing the victim to sign assets over to the perpetrator or to enable access to line of credit.[15]

In 2021 I led a research project funded by the Australian Institute of Criminology, during which we interviewed 170 victim-survivors of coercive control living in Australia. Numerous victim-survivors shared horrific stories of the coercive and controlling abuse they had experienced from their partners, including financial abuse. It was during this project that I interviewed Ash. She described in detail her experience of financial abuse by her then husband:

> If you have a joint account, having to ask permission to spend money. And it can be so insidious and subtle … like, 'Sure just spend it on whatever you want.' And in my situation, I asked if I could have money on a monthly basis, so I could just spend it. And it was like, 'No, no. Just use the joint account.' But anything I spent money on was then queried. My ex used to work away on rosters and he used to have this opinion that, why was the water bill so high? Why was the food bill so high? Why was the power bill so high? And he had this

> thing where even though the money being spent was for his partner of then fifteen years and then wife and his children, he shouldn't have to pay that because he worked away and he wasn't there. And yet he'd come home and he'd leave the tap running and the lights on and complain at everyone else. 'You're always leaving the lights on and you're costing so much money.' Things like, 'I need a new pair of jeans. Is it alright if I buy some jeans?' 'You've got a cupboard full of clothes.' … He drained me of over $200 000 in my savings … I wasn't allowed to work, that was just, 'No, you're not working.' … And if you ever did have the courage to do something out of line, because you live in fear, constant fear, the ramifications of that were just not worth doing something wrong. The massive rages and explosions followed by the silent treatment.

For Amy, another victim-survivor interviewed as part of the coercive control project, her experience of financial abuse continued beyond the relationship and into the period of separation. Amy, aged in her forties and living in New South Wales, described how her partner:

> kicked me out of my job, because we had a business together and he kicked me out of that, so I had no job, no income, and he made me pay the whole mortgage because I was living here but … he wouldn't sign

> paperwork to change the mortgage to interest only while we were going through four years of family law court. So somehow, I had to pay the full mortgage by myself that whole time with no job and no income.

Amy and Ash's experiences illustrate the lived reality of economic and financial abuse—the ways in which an abuser utilises their control over their partner to whittle away at their financial decision-making and independence, and thereby their safety. Over the past decade of conducting research on coercive control, I have heard numerous stories like these.

A current parliamentary inquiry has provided a political platform for victim-survivors of this form of abuse to share their experiences. The Financial Services Regulatory Framework in Relation to Financial Abuse inquiry has heard calls for a range of reforms to the operation of financial institutions, including the major banks and other lending organisations, to more effectively identify, prevent and, if needed, respond to this form of abuse. These calls are welcome, but while our understanding of abuse and the myriad ways in which it can be perpetrated is expanding, domestic, family and sexual violence are old problems that are showing no sign of abating.

These acts of male violence must not continue to be the everyday experiences of women and girls across Australia, but they are.

CHILDREN AS VICTIM-SURVIVORS IN THEIR OWN RIGHT

Our evolving understandings of violence at the state and national levels has included the need to improve awareness of, and responses to, child victims. The recently released *National Plan to End Violence against Women and Children, 2022–2032*,[16] recognises children as victim-survivors of domestic, family and sexual violence in their own right. Moving from symbolic recognition to meaningful actions and solutions requires quantification of the problem. While prevalence data on adult victimisation has been gathered for some time now, we have only in recent years begun to measure at scale the prevalence of abuse experienced by children in Australia.

In 2023, the landmark Australian Child Maltreatment Study found that experiences of child maltreatment, including physical abuse, sexual abuse, emotional abuse and neglect, are widespread among the Australian population. The study found that among Australians aged 16–65 years old, 32 per cent experienced physical abuse during childhood; 28.5 per cent experienced sexual abuse during childhood; 31 per cent experienced emotional abuse during childhood; and 9 per cent experienced neglect during childhood.[17] Reflecting the gendered nature of violence, the study also found that girls are at greater risk of experiencing most types of maltreatment, including higher rates of both sexual and emotional abuse. Specifically, one in three Australian girls experience child sexual abuse, and girls experience double the rate of child sexual abuse that boys endure.[18]

In many instances, Australian children experience abuse on more than one occasion. The study found that instances of child sexual abuse, for example, are rarely experienced once by a child victim. Horrifically, for 11 per cent of children in this study, acts of child sexual abuse happened more than fifty times. The level of harm involved is indescribable.

The killing of children in the context of domestic and family violence is devastatingly common. Filicide—the term used to describe a child being killed by their parent—is the second most common type of domestic homicide in Australia. In 2024, a report produced by ANROWS, a national research body on violence against women, showed that in the vast majority of Australian filicide cases (76 per cent), there is a history of domestic and family violence, including child abuse and/or intimate partner violence. In particular, in cases where a father killed their child or children, this typically followed a history of the father's perpetration of intimate partner violence.

This is thought to have been the case with Arthur Freeman, who was convicted of the 2009 murder of his four-year-old daughter Darcey in Victoria. In a killing that horrified the country, in the midst of a child custody dispute, Freeman threw his daughter off the West Gate Bridge in Melbourne. Chief Crown prosecutor Gavin Silbert SC submitted at trial that Freeman was solely and entirely motivated by a desire for spousal revenge.[19]

The ANROWS report includes a clear call to action: 'We need to see and respond to children as victims of domestic and family violence in their own right. Failure can be fatal.'[20] This failure is most acutely evident when we look to the lives of First Nations children in Australia.

FIRST NATIONS COMMUNITIES: ACKNOWLEDGING SYSTEMIC FAILURES

While domestic, family and sexual violence is present across *all* Australian communities, there are some community groups that are impacted more heavily than others, and some women who face a greater risk of violence. It is essential to acknowledge the significant impact that violence has on First Nations communities across Australia. Aboriginal and Torres Strait Islander women experience all forms of family and domestic violence at significantly higher rates than non-Indigenous Australians. Indeed, Indigenous women are twice as likely as non-Indigenous women to be killed by an intimate partner, and they are up to thirty-two times more likely to be hospitalised as a result of domestic and family violence.[21]

Every time I recall these statistics, I am confounded by the everyday violent reality of Indigenous women's lives. During the writing of this book, the Yoorrook Justice Commission, the first formal truth-telling process focused on the historical and ongoing injustices experienced by First Nations people in Victoria, completed its public hearings into the criminal justice system, child protection system, housing, health and economic prosperity. The hearings were streamed live online, and I felt compelled to watch them. I felt an intense responsibility to listen and learn, to reflect, and to commit to being part of the solution in whatever way I can.

The hearings laid bare the clear reality that Victoria's family violence system has failed First Nations women and children. In her opening comments to the commission as part of the social justice hearings, Victorian Minister for Prevention of Family Violence Vicki Ward said:

> I also acknowledge that historically the systems that have been designed to keep women safe from family violence have been marked by discrimination and systemic racism. They have failed to listen to First Peoples women and have failed to keep First Peoples women and children safe ... I apologise to First Peoples victim survivors, families and community and those directly affected by family violence.[22]

This was one of many apologies provided by state government members to the commissioners throughout the public hearings.

The Yoorrook Justice Commission is led by five commissioners, among them Deputy Chair Sue-Anne Hunter, a Wurundjeri woman, social worker and advocate committed to improving the rights of Aboriginal children and families. Three years ago, at the 2021 March4Justice in Naarm (Melbourne), I had the honour of listening to her powerful call to action. Standing in the Treasury Gardens among thousands of advocates and change-makers, I listened as Sue-Anne said:

> Aboriginal women have fought against gendered violence perpetrated by white men since day one. The allegations, cover up and silence on gendered violence in federal parliament is part of the same system of abuse and the same lack of legal and political consequences. Enough is Enough.[23]

Indeed, enough is enough. As a white Australian woman, I recognise my complicity, and that of the generations before me. I know that the colonial brutality in our history has a lot to answer for here, and I am grateful to live in Victoria where the process of truth and treaty is providing a First Nations–forged space in which to acknowledge those harms. I am also acutely aware that as a criminologist, I have studied in detail the very systems of justice that have been sites of significant harm for First Nations communities, and I understand that the push over the last three decades to toughen criminal justice system responses to men's violence against women, while often well intentioned, has exacerbated these harms. Strategies to criminalise violence against women have had disproportionate impacts on Aboriginal and Torres Strait Islander communities, which are over-policed and disproportionately incarcerated.[24]

I know that there are no quick-fix solutions here, but I also absolutely recognise that if we are to find lasting solutions, it will be by listening to First Nations communities and upholding their self-determination in processes of policy and practice reform.

In 2022, I was fortunate to lead a team of researchers who conducted national stakeholder consultations to inform the development of Australia's *National Plan to End Violence against Women and Children, 2022–2032.* My team had the privilege of hearing from First Nations elders, community leaders, practitioners and victim-survivor advocates. Throughout those consultations, the importance of community interventions that are led by First Nations people, and which are culturally sensitive and safe, was emphasised. We repeatedly heard that those who have the political power to do so must direct the required resources to First Nations communities so that they can themselves develop and deliver the prevention and response interventions needed to meaningfully and appropriately address all forms of domestic, family and sexual violence that affect their communities.

THE COVID-19 PANDEMIC

The once in a lifetime (let's hope!) events of the last five years necessitate an acknowledgement of the impact of the COVID-19 pandemic on the nature and frequency of men's violence against women. Shortly after the outbreak of the virus, the executive director of United Nations Women, Phumzile Mlambo-Ngcuka, labelled violence against women the 'shadow pandemic'. The declaration provided a label to describe what many, including myself, already feared: that family, domestic and sexual violence would be exacerbated during the pandemic. Deepening this concern, in early April 2020, as the virus rapidly spread and countries worldwide entered into varying degrees of government-enforced lockdown, the United Nations Population Fund predicted that for every three months of such lockdowns, an additional fifteen million cases of domestic violence would occur globally—yes, fifteen million *additional* cases.

During the first two years of the pandemic, I had the opportunity to work as part of a Monash University research team to understand how the public health measures invoked to combat the spread of COVID were impacting interpersonal safety in Australia and access to the relevant support services. Our research showed that the pandemic exacerbated women's experiences of intimate partner violence, in relation to both the frequency and the severity of the violence experienced.[25] We also documented the ways in which abusers weaponised the pandemic to perpetrate new forms of abusive behaviours within their relationships. For example, in our 2020 Monash-led Victorian research speaking with family violence specialist workers, one practitioner described how perpetrators were:

> Demanding women … wash their hands and body excessively to a point [where] women's skin starts to bleed and become badly irritated; spreading a vicious rumour she's got COVID-19 so nobody would come near her or help her; taking children away saying she is likely to have/get COVID-19 and is a risk to children.[26]

This is not to suggest that the coronavirus in and of itself caused violence against women. The link is absolutely not causal—responsibility for violence lies first and firmly with the individuals who choose to use violence. But the COVID-19 pandemic certainly provided the conditions within which men's violence against women could flourish. During periods of lockdown, deemed necessary from a public health perspective, women and children were isolated more than ever before, access to formal and informal supports were minimised, and financial stresses increased—all of which lent an enormous degree of irony to the oft-repeated government mantra 'Stay home, stay safe'. Needless to say, the mental health stresses on individuals and families during this time have been well documented, as have the concerning impacts of the pandemic years on children and young people. There is also awareness that while international borders are no longer closed as a quarantine measure, and the use of lockdowns has well and truly passed, for many Australians with long COVID, the troubling intersection between intimate partner violence and health continues.

In early 2024, I led a study with Monash colleagues that for the first time worldwide asked the question: what happens when a person is experiencing long COVID and intimate partner violence at the same time?[27] While we know that victim-survivors of intimate partner violence are twice as likely to develop long-term illnesses, including chronic fatigue syndrome and fibromyalgia,[28] our study sought to reveal the previously unseen impacts of long COVID on individuals experiencing intimate partner violence.

The World Health Organization (WHO) defines long COVID as the continuation of existing symptoms, or the development of new ones, three months after the initial COVID infection. Global studies estimate that one in ten infected people go on to develop long COVID symptoms. A review conducted by the Australian Institute of Health and Welfare found that middle-aged adult women in Australia were at higher risk of experiencing severe COVID-19, as were individuals with comorbidities.[29] Like the initial infection, symptoms of long COVID include respiratory issues, cognitive dysfunction, and fatigue—all of which can impact a person's everyday functioning.

Drawing from the experiences of twenty-eight Australians who had long COVID and had also experienced intimate partner violence, the Monash study found that each of these conditions worsened an individual's experience of the other. For example, one woman we surveyed explained:

> I think the illness on top of my other conditions made him perceive me as more of a burden, leading to poor behaviour. There were a few signs of this prior to my having COVID, but I think my being vulnerable when I had previously been the 'strong' and 'independent' partner really threw him off and he rejected that.[30]

Another victim-survivor put the rapid increase in abuse they experienced down to the difficult social conditions of living through lockdowns and in isolation, describing how the pandemic 'gave us too much time to know so much about each other. That worsened the abusive tendencies.'

Victim-survivors we heard from in this study also described how their partners weaponised or manipulated their long COVID symptoms to carry out abusive behaviours. Perpetrators exploited the mental and physical effects of long COVID to further entrap victim-survivors in coercively controlling relationships. The impacts on victim-survivors were significant, with individuals describing simultaneously losing control of their health and their safety since contracting long COVID. This is a key area of risk and need that we cannot lose sight of in the months and years to come.

Reinforcing this is the body of work in Australia that has consistently found that women with chronic health conditions and disability are at significantly higher risk of experiencing all forms of violence, including intimate partner violence.[31] Recognition of the higher risk that women with disability are exposed to has been accompanied by increased recognition of the unique forms of abuse perpetrated against women with disability. This includes where a perpetrator restricts or withholds aids or medications; refuses to provide assistance with personal care tasks, such as using the bathroom or dressing; forces involuntary sterilisation or pregnancy termination; or refuses access to finances to pay for treatment.[32]

THE IMPACTS OF DOMESTIC AND FAMILY VIOLENCE

As I have already begun to explain, the impacts of domestic and family violence are significant, wide-ranging, immediate, and can be long-lasting.

The WHO has written extensively on this topic, providing an exhaustive list of the lived legacy of abuse for victims, including the health consequences, the social and economic costs, and the physical, emotional and psychological impacts, as well as the immediate and long-term—if not lifelong—impacts on children.[33]

Importantly, it is now widely recognised that the effects of abuse extend far beyond the point in time at which the abuse takes place. They can infiltrate all facets of a victim-survivors' everyday life. Research shows that the experience of living in a state of constant fear and hypervigilance heavily impacts victim-survivors' mental and physical health. Victim-survivors of intimate partner violence also experience high levels of post-traumatic stress disorder, sleep disorders, depression and anxiety, as well as physical disabilities.

Listening to and learning from individuals with lived experience of intimate partner violence has crystallised for me the impacts of abuse. Countless victim-survivors have described to me the impacts of coercive control as worse than any single incident of physical harm enacted during the term of their abusive relationships.

Ava is a Victorian woman aged in her forties. When I interviewed her in 2021, she told me that:

> having endured twelve years of it [abuse], do you know what? The psychological and coercive control is far, far, far worse than being hit. I've had both. And the

> coercive control and the manipulation and intimidation is a thousand times worse than the physical.

Research on the impacts of abuse is continually evolving. Just this year, one of the first Australian studies on the impacts of intimate partner violence on a victim's brain identified two women with the degenerative brain disease chronic traumatic encephalopathy, or CTE.[34] Up until now, this condition has been more commonly associated with males playing contact sports, such as American football, wrestling, boxing and rugby. This recent discovery adds to our understanding of the long-term impacts of physical intimate partner violence.

Just as for adults, the impacts of abuse during childhood are significant. Child victim-survivors are at increased risk of poor mental health, suicide, disengagement from school, disability and other chronic health problems. In Australia, family violence remains the leading cause of youth homelessness, while death by suicide is the leading cause of death among 15–24-year-olds. As Australia's *National Plan to End Violence against Women and Children, 2022–2032* states: 'A child's worldview is shaped by the violence they see, hear and experience each day. These experiences affect their perception and understanding of the world, which can have long-term and ongoing impacts.'[35]

With this quote in mind, it is perhaps unsurprising that violence can be intergenerational. This is not to suggest that all children who are abused will go on to perpetrate violence. It is simply a recognition that among those who do use violence, there is a high likelihood that they experienced violence first themselves.

Research I led with Australian colleagues found that one in two young people who experience domestic and family violence during childhood go on to use violence in the home also during their childhood.[36] Specifically, our survey of 5000 young Australians aged sixteen to twenty years old found that of those young people who report using violence in the home during adolescence, almost nine in ten report childhood experiences of domestic and family violence, and other forms of child maltreatment. One eighteen-year-old female surveyed for this study, reflected: 'My own behaviour felt like a mirror of the behaviour I experienced which I hated, but I didn't know how to break the cycle because regardless of how I changed my behaviour, I still experienced the same abuse.'[37]

Among those young people in our study who reported using domestic and family violence, the most common forms were verbal abuse, physical violence and emotional/psychological abuse. Such evidence reminds us that the impacts of trauma and the lived experience of these young people must be at the heart of earlier intervention and prevention strategies.

More broadly, and looking across the range of impacts of abuse, it is critical that we fully understand the complexity and far-ranging nature of the injuries and impacts of intimate partner violence, in order for the relevant services to be truly responsive and effective in supporting the needs of victims of abuse—and not just in times of immediate crisis needs. These services and associated systems must be designed to recognise and respond to the impacts experienced long after a victim leaves an abusive relationship.

This brings us to a key point in better understanding the full range of impacts, particularly in relation to intimate partner violence: expanded knowledge of coercive control.

WHAT IS COERCIVE CONTROL?

The term 'coercive control' has a history in clinical settings. It first originated about fifteen years ago in the United States, popularised by American sociologist and forensic social worker Evan Stark.[38] Since then, in Australia and elsewhere across the world, including the United Kingdom, United States and Canada, coercive control has become part of the vernacular. The term is used to capture the pattern of abuse that a perpetrator enacts on a victim—most often a female intimate partner—including social, financial, psychological and technology-facilitated abuse. In their research on Australian women's experiences of coercive control for the Australian Institute of Criminology, Hayley Boxall and Anthony Morgan found that the most commonly experienced forms were jealousy and suspicion of friends, constant insults, monitoring of movements and financial abuse.[39] When these abusive behaviours are enacted together as a pattern of control and coercion perpetrated over time, coercive control represents a form of abuse that is often targeted at dismantling the core independence of the victim.

It has been argued that decades of focusing on individual incidents of physical violence have obscured a full appreciation of the ongoing patterns of abuse that women can suffer. The everyday reality of living with violence that is experienced by those within coercive and controlling relationships may be difficult to fully comprehend for anyone who has not experienced it first-hand. Compounding this lack of understanding is the fact that coercive control can involve patterns of abusive behaviours that cannot be readily identified. There may be no bruises or other physical marks in evidence. Rather, it is often the internal core of the individual woman that is impacted, and dramatically so.

The NSW Domestic Violence Death Review Team found that coercive and controlling behaviours were perpetrated in a relationship prior to over 90 per cent of intimate partner homicides in that state between 2008 and 2016.[40] This is not a finding unique to intimate partner killings in New South Wales. An analysis of domestic violence–related deaths in the Australian Capital Territory likewise found that prior coercive and controlling behaviours were evident in almost every case.[41] Such reviews highlight why a focus on addressing coercive control is critically needed. Patterns of coercive and controlling behaviours are a significant threat to the day-to-day wellbeing, quality of life and safety of Australian women and children.

Perpetrators are skilled in manipulation. Abusive behaviours are enacted over time at levels of intensity and in varying forms such that it can be extremely difficult for the targeted victim to anticipate or decipher. The frog in boiling water metaphor is terribly apt here. If a frog is placed in a pot of lukewarm water that is slowly heated to boiling point, it will not perceive the gradual increase in temperature as dangerous. The frog will remain in the water, adjusting to the slow rise in heat until it eventually reaches a lethal temperature.

The fatal consequences of coercive and controlling relationships confronted the Australian public following the horrific killing of Hannah Clarke and her three children: Aaliyah, Laianah and Trey. Hannah's estranged husband, Rowan Baxter, ambushed Hannah and her three children when she was driving to school on the morning of 19 February 2020. Baxter dowsed the family car in petrol and a short time later set it alight, killing the children. Hannah died that afternoon from injuries sustained in the attack.[42]

Following Hannah's death, it was reported that she had experienced years of coercive and controlling behaviour from her husband and eventual killer. Hannah's mother, Sue Clarke, said:

> He always knew where Hannah was. He would turn up at places quite expectedly, and she would notice her handbag or phone had been rifled through. He would ring her when she should be locking up the gym, to see if she had locked up on time and if there was anyone there with her. He would control what she wore. Hannah was never allowed to wear pink or shorts … He would also control what the children did, and he would force sex on Hannah every night and if she didn't comply, he would sulk for days.[43]

What Sue describes here are the controlling behaviours all too commonly experienced by women in abusive intimate-partner relationships. They are the day-to-day tactics used by perpetrators in their attempts to fully control the lives of their partners, whittling away at their sense of independence.

The Queensland coronial inquest into the killing of Hannah and her children further documented the significant history of coercive control that preceded the murders. Coronial inquests are used to investigate the circumstances and causes of sudden, unnatural or unexplained deaths, and to make recommendations to prevent similar deaths in the future. Over two weeks, the inquest into the killing of Hannah Clarke heard from numerous witnesses who documented the range of coercive and controlling behaviours present in the relationship with Baxter.[44]

The abusive behaviours recounted included jealousy and attempts to isolate Hannah from her friends—these were evident from the outset of her relationship with Baxter. The inquiry heard that after they began living together, Hannah was told by Baxter that she was not allowed to wear shorts, short skirts or the colour pink, and that while she could wear a bikini at the beach, she should not wear one anywhere else. The inquest also heard that over the course of the relationship, family and friends had witnessed Baxter openly criticising members of Hannah's family, and preventing her and their children from attending family events. The inquest was told it was likely that Baxter had installed a listening device in their house and another in Hannah's car, given the number of times he had revealed knowledge of events and conversations for which he had not been present. Compounding this surveillance, Baxter apparently used to check Hannah's phone while she slept, and over time he became suspicious that she was having an extramarital affair.

Taken on their own, any one of these behaviours could be explained away or excused by family and friends who do not see the full range of coercive and controlling behaviours being enacted. However, as the inquest into the deaths of Hannah Clarke and her children so brutally reminds us, there is a need to better understand how such behaviours intersect, and how they represent a key warning sign that a woman is at risk of serious harm or death.

OPPORTUNITIES FOR INTERVENTION

The coronial inquest into the killing of Hannah Clarke and her three children also examined questions surrounding the effectiveness of civil and criminal justice system responses to men's violence against women. At the time of her death, Hannah had a civil protection order in place against her estranged husband. Baxter had been charged with breaching the domestic violence order weeks before and was due to appear in court. Hannah had met with a former police officer to prepare a safety plan.[45]

I remember reading the details of Hannah's life and experiences of abuse in absolute despair. Here was a woman who had tried to seek safety for her children and herself, away from a coercive and controlling relationship, and yet they were murdered. This despite the fact that numerous professionals, family members and friends were aware of Baxter's abusive behaviour towards Hannah. The killings of Hannah, Aaliyah, Laianah and Trey starkly illustrate how much work is still needed to effectively address the risk of future harm from men's violence—to ensure the safety of the victims, and to ultimately prevent their deaths.

This has been a key focus of my research over the last five years, working in collaboration with a brilliant team from Monash University. We recently published the findings from our analysis of 235 cases of male-perpetrated intimate partner femicide subject to sentencing in an Australian court over a decade.[46] For this study, we read in detail the comments made by judges during the sentencing of men who had killed their female partners (current and former), in order to better understand the known risks, and the points at which the victim and perpetrator had interacted with different points of the family violence and justice systems prior to the killing. We wanted to identify as many opportunities as possible for preventing such killings.

Our research found that many of these deaths could have been prevented. The majority of the perpetrators had known histories of violence, and in many cases, different points of the system were aware of the violence within the intimate partner relationship. Over the cases we studied, 65 per cent of offenders had been convicted of a criminal offence before they killed their female partner, and 34 per cent had a prior conviction for a domestic violence–related incident. This shows that for a majority of offenders, lethal violence against women does not come 'out of the blue', but rather represents a continuation and escalation of the violence previously used.

One of the homicide cases in our study was that of 43-year-old Victorian woman Kelly Thompson, who was killed in February 2014 by her former partner Wayne Wood.[47] In the months before Kelly's death, Wood had at least twice breached an intervention order she had taken out against him, and he had also repeatedly threatened violence against Kelly, along with incidents where he stalked and tried to strangle her. In the three weeks before she was killed, Kelly called the police on at least thirty-five occasions and also disclosed the violence to friends, neighbours and work colleagues. Only a few hours before she was killed, Kelly's neighbour called the police to report that Wood was at Kelly's house and acting strangely; he also told the police that he believed Wood was in breach of an intervention order. But the police officer who took that call did not check to see if there was an intervention order in place, nor did he send police to the house. Instead, the officer asked the neighbour: 'Can you do me a massive favour pal and keep an eye on the address? If you hear any yelling or screaming from the address, I'll send a van around to have a look.'[48]

Recalling that response elicits the same reaction in me every time. Is this really the best we can do? Three hours after her neighbour contacted the police, Kelly was stabbed to death and Wood subsequently died by suicide. Another woman, desperately trying to get help to secure her own safety, killed by men's violence.

The coronial inquest held into Kelly's death found that police oversights meant that serious threats to her safety were not recognised or acted upon. While the coroner was careful not to imply that anyone but Wayne Wood was responsible for Kelly Thompson's death, he did find that the police response 'fell short', and pointed to the absence of a proper risk assessment, a lack of police understanding of intimate partner violence, a number of missed opportunities to intervene, and the limitations of information-sharing provisions between police and family violence agencies.[49]

For me, the circumstances surrounding Kelly's death so clearly capture many of the failings in our family violence system, particularly around comprehensive responses and the need for effective risk assessment and management practices. While Kelly Thompson was killed a decade ago now, and acknowledging that there has been significant reform in the intervening ten years—particularly in Victoria—it is harrowing to know that many of the flaws in system responses to men's violence against women remain across Australia's states and territories. We simply must do better. This requires substantive resourcing to provide more specialist domestic and family violence–informed training, and coordinated system responses underpinned by solid data-sharing and shared understandings of how to effectively identify, assess and respond to risk. There's my wish list of what is needed, but more on that in the final sections of this book.

The circumstances of Kelly's killing, among others, are an alarming indication that justice system responses to violence may not be effective in preventing serious harm or death. But at the same time, I urge caution in how we respond. We will not be able to arrest or jail our way out of this problem, and any reforms to expand the reach and powers of the criminal justice system will always have disproportionate and in many cases harmful impacts on marginalised groups such as First Nations communities.

The criminal justice system is a blunt tool, reactive by nature, not preventative. If we wait until victims call the police, or until police intervention is required, then we are simply accepting that intimate partner violence will occur. We are resigning ourselves to always becoming involved after the fact. What I am calling for here is a commitment to earlier intervention and prevention. While there is a critical need for an effective and well-funded response system, given the scale of the crisis, we must ensure it does not come at the cost of investing in efforts at prevention.

The circumstances of deaths such as those of Kelly remind us that women's deaths from male violence are preventable—in hindsight, we see the opportunities for prevention time and time again. In some cases, they are preventable because the systemic failings that contributed to a woman's death are identifiable and *should* be rectifiable. In other cases, they are preventable by virtue of the number of known risk factors present in the victim's life prior to the act of femicide. All too often, when I look back through the lives of the women killed by men's violence, the number of different services and systems that had only a partial perspective on the woman victim or the male perpetrator becomes apparent. The challenge for those responsible for system design and resourcing is how to ensure that the visibility of these risks translates into effective risk assessment and management, and more effective and earlier intervention.

PREVENTING CHILDREN'S DEATHS IN A SYSTEM DESIGNED FOR ADULTS

Children's deaths in the context of domestic and family violence are preventable. But prevention and early intervention are not consistently achievable within our current approaches, policies and practices, which routinely overlook the safety needs of, and risks faced by, children as victim-survivors in their own right. Children can feel invisible in the systems where they seek help, responded to merely as an extension of a protective parent as opposed to being recognised in their own right. Writing shortly after the release of the *National*

Plan to End Violence against Women and Children, 2022–2032, Professor Silke Meyer and I described the impact of system responses that fail to see children from this perspective:

> we fail to recognise and adequately respond to children's unique safety, support and recovery needs. This can make children invisible in relevant risk assessment; assessors may miss the specific risk to children's safety and wellbeing in the context of domestic and family violence. This can lead to preventable harm, injury or even homicide and suicide.

Policy and practice reform is urgently needed.

In 2023, I had the absolute honour of leading a research project that involved conducting interviews with seventeen Victorian children and young people who had experienced family violence and accessed the family violence system. The children and young people whom we spoke with were incredibly insightful as to what was needed to improve responses to child victims of domestic and family violence, and they were abundantly clear in their assessment of current system responses: all the young people we interviewed were unanimous in describing the inadequacy of current responses.

While incredibly disappointing, this response was also sadly predictable. Governments in Australia have repeatedly failed to recognise and adequately respond to the unique safety, support and recovery needs of the individual child. In 2016, the Victorian Royal Commission into Family Violence described children as the 'silent victims' of family violence.[50] Five years later, in 2021, the *Now You Have Heard Us, What Will You Do?* report led by the ACT Children and Young People Commissioner concluded that the voices of children and young people are often missing from the decisions that impact upon their lives.[51]

This year marks the tenth anniversary of the murder of Luke Batty—a killing that transformed conversations on domestic and family violence in Australia. In February 2014, in an act of premeditated violence, Luke was beaten and stabbed to death by his father, Greg Anderson, at cricket practice in the outer-Melbourne suburb of Tyabb. The coronial inquest into Luke's killing found there had been a series of 'missed opportunities' to intervene in the case, and that numerous organisations had been ineffectual in only partially identifying the risk Luke faced.[52]

The day after her son was murdered by her estranged partner, Rosie Batty spoke to the waiting media in front of her house, and her words cut through the problem of domestic and family violence in an intensely powerful way:

> I want to tell people that family violence happens to [anybody], no matter how nice your house is, no matter

> how intelligent you are. When you're involved with family violence, friends, family judge you, the woman—the decisions you should make, the decisions you don't make. You're the victim, but you become the person that people condemn ... What I want people to take from this is that it isn't simple. People judge you, people tell you what you should do. You do the best you can.[53]

Each time I recall Rosie's words, I am struck by their power. At the time, the public reaction to them seemed to indicate that Rosie's message was being heard, that Australia might finally and fully *get it*. In 2015 she was named Australian of the Year, and over the next twelve months she spoke at over 250 public events and attended countless meetings with federal, state and territory politicians. Rosie was ever-present in the media and, as a result, the issue of domestic and family violence was ever-present in the national conversation in a way that I'd never seen before. Rosie's advocacy and the outrage provoked by Luke's death has also been credited as a significant impetus behind the establishment of the Royal Commission into Family Violence, Australia's first (and so far its only) such royal commission.

I was extremely privileged to be part of two events with Rosie to mark the tenth anniversary of Luke's death, and also the publication of her book *Hope*.[54] Rosie's perspective and strength a decade on from the horrific murder of her son amazes me. She is so gracious in highlighting the progress that has been made, but her approach should not be mistaken as an acceptance of the status quo. As Rosie and I wrote in a joint article earlier this year, it is unfathomable that despite a decade of increased political attention and reform, many of the recommendations of the coronial inquiry into Luke's killing—Victoria-specific at the time, but nationally relevant and critically needed across all Australian states and territories—have not been enacted. Why do children continue to fall off the national and state policy agendas relating to domestic, family and sexual violence?

FAILURES OF THE JUSTICE SYSTEM

In among assessments of the adequacy of current policies and practice, it is important to recognise that many victim-survivors do not seek a punitive response. For them, *not reporting* to the police is a deliberate decision. This may stem from a desire to remain with the abuser, but to do so safely and without harm; a decision to focus on crisis needs and recovery supports; or indeed, it may reflect the lack of confidence that many victim-survivors have in our police and court system.

In our Monash research involving interviews with Australian victim-survivors of coercive control, many individuals spoke to us about their lack of confidence in the justice system as well as the myriad ways in which engagement with the system had re-traumatised them.

For these women, the perpetrator was their first abuser, and the justice system their second.

Janine, a woman aged in her forties and living in Victoria, recounted to us her experience reporting intimate partner violence to the police:

> I've been laughed at. I've been laughed out of police stations, I've been told that I'm overreacting, I've been told that it's just guys being guys, or that he's just got a bit het up and he just needs to calm down, that that's what guys do. I can think of one specific police station I just walked out of in tears. They made me feel so bad for going there, and I could get this guy into trouble, he's a professional. Do I want to do that? It's just—yeah. I would never have believed it if I hadn't experienced it. And the same with some courts. Yeah, it took me a very, very long time … I think three tries, to get an intervention order.

Vera, a Victorian woman in her sixties, explained that 'the trauma that's involved with the court system means that eventually the woman's so traumatised she'll just give up because she can't do it'.

What Vera described is not justice by any imagination.

It takes victim-survivors immense courage to report to police and navigate the legal system. When they do so, they should not confront a failure to secure their safety, nor an experience that may retraumatise them. But in many ways, this is not surprising. Let's not forget—the justice system was made by men and for men, and as victim-survivor accounts often remind us, it continues to serve the dominant interests of men.

That said, while a significant amount of work remains to be done to address the failures in our criminal justice system's responses to domestic, family and sexual violence, I do want to acknowledge the countless individuals across Australia working tirelessly to improve the system—from those who work within to effect change, to those who champion change from the outside.

BEYOND MERELY SURVIVING TO THRIVING

Regardless of whether a victim-survivor decides to report to police or not, there is a need to also ensure we have broader support services in place to support the recovery and healing needs of the victim.

A strong focus on recovery and healing for victims of domestic, family and sexual violence is long overdue and deeply needed. I have already detailed the consequences of abuse—they are profound, impacting upon every aspect of an individual's life both in the short term and the long term. The effects of abuse can also be exacerbated during the period of relationship separation. Victim-survivors often suffer immense financial loss, including lost property and assets, when they leave an abusive relationship.

Unsurprisingly, as research by Anne Summers has shown, the financial impacts of abuse are heightened for single mothers, who are at high risk of living beneath the poverty line within five years of leaving their abusive partner. Let that sit with you for a moment—the fact that in Australia, women who choose a life of non-violence, who set that example for their children, confront the real risk of living in poverty within a few years of escaping an abuser. As Summers so aptly summarised in her report, this is 'The Choice', between violence and poverty—one that far too many Australian women continue to face in 2024.

There is some hope of an end to the policy vacuum here. Australia's *National Plan to End Violence against Women and Children, 2022–2032* includes a ground-breaking focus on recovery and healing. Included as one of four domains, this focus aims to break the cycle of violence and reduce the risk of re-traumatisation for victim-survivors of domestic, family and sexual violence. This represents a pivotal shift, whereby the Australian Government has committed to delivering a systems-based response that is not based on the premise that if you survive the violence experienced, then the job is done, but rather invites a reimagined and expanded response that supports victim-survivors to thrive beyond the violence experienced.

Delivering on this means providing much more support for victim-survivors' physical and mental health, and economic and social recovery—all facets of an individual's life that are deeply impacted by abuse. Importantly, supporting women's financial independence must begin well before a woman leaves an abusive relationship, and is a crucial component of equal pay and broader gender equality initiatives underway across Australia. Women's financial insecurity has significant impacts on their safety. We often hear someone ask the problematic question: 'Why didn't she just leave?' But often, leaving is not an option for women, particularly so where their economic independence has been eroded by the perpetrator. Research in Australia and overseas has consistently found that women who are financially independent are better positioned to leave an abusive male partner, and to remain separated from them in the long term.[55] Financial insecurity must be understood both as an impact of an abusive relationship as well as a key barrier to achieving safety and freedom from that violence.

BLAMING WOMEN FOR MEN'S VIOLENCE

There is another important point to make here. That question—'Why didn't she just leave?'—is problematic for many reasons, several of which I've already discussed. But a point I haven't yet made is the way in which it places the responsibility onto the victim themselves. You may as well ask, 'Why didn't she keep herself safe?' When such a question is asked, no matter the caveats attached to it, it is the behaviour of the victim that is deemed at fault, while the actions of the perpetrator—and their own responsibility to stop using violence—are diminished.

Victim-blaming, which contributes to a lack of perpetrator accountability for men's violence against women, is an issue of profound significance for me. It is the reason that I embarked on a PhD in criminology at Monash University in early 2008. Having originally enrolled in university with the hopes of becoming an actress, I followed my interests throughout my undergraduate degree in arts into majors in criminology and psychology. Then, when the opportunity presented itself for me to undertake a year of research as part of an honours degree in criminology, I jumped into it, completely unaware of where it might lead. A year later, when invited to enrol in a PhD in criminology, my niggling sense of injustice over one particular case drove me to choose a very specific topic, and propelled me into a research journey that continues to this day.

Four years prior to starting my PhD, I—like many Victorians—had watched in disbelief as James Ramage was convicted and sentenced to eleven years' jail for the manslaughter of his estranged wife Julie. To me, the sentence imposed seemed outrageously lenient, and the label of manslaughter wholly inadequate given

Ramage's lethal actions. Coupled with this, the highly problematic victim-blaming message sent by the court, and magnified by the media's coverage of the case, struck me as manifestly unjust. The clear injustice of this case has been a motivator for a significant portion of my career to date.

In July 2003, Julie Ramage met with her estranged husband James at their previously shared family home in Melbourne to discuss renovation plans. Julie and James had been separated for five weeks following a twenty-year marriage during which they had two children, Matthew and Samantha. Of course, in understanding what happened between Julie and James at their final meeting, there is only James's version of events, put forward in his trial defence. I'll leave you to extrapolate the implications of that.

James alleged that Julie dismissed the significance of the progress of the renovations, and that, responding to his plea that she return to the marriage, she told him that sex with him 'repulsed her and screwed up her face and either said or implied how much better her new [boy] friend was'.[56] James then claimed that he lost control and fatally attacked Julie. His subsequent actions were described by the judge as an act 'of immediate and overwhelming brutality by a man considerably larger and physically stronger than his victim'.[57]

There is a long list of details that makes James Ramage's crime abhorrent, but what I want to focus on here is the injustice of the response by the courts. James did not deny that he had killed his wife. The trial concentrated on the level of his responsibility in doing so—specifically, the question of whether, in the time immediately prior to her death, Julie's actions had provoked her estranged husband and caused him to lose his self-control and inflict lethal violence. Yes, it was *her* actions, and not his fatal abusive behaviours, that were given primary attention throughout the trial.

Witnesses were called to provide evidence of James's coercive and controlling behaviour towards Julie throughout their marriage. Acts of intimidation, forced sex, alleged physical violence and threats of violence were described.[58] The prosecution used this evidence to make the case that Julie had held 'a continuing underlying fear' of James, and that it was unlikely that she would have said the words attributed to her by James during the pair's final meeting.[59] Much of this evidence, however, was not heard by the jury. It was deemed highly prejudicial and subject to hearsay.[60] The evidence presented by the defence, which was heard by the jury, told a vastly different story.

James's defence sought to shift responsibility onto Julie by invoking victim-blaming narratives. One argument by the defence counsel has stayed with me for what is now over twenty years. It deftly illustrates all that is wrong not just with this case but with the way in which we blame women victims of intimate partner violence in Australia. The defence introduced evidence that Julie had a tampon on her person at the time of her death, This, they put to the jury, supported their claim that she started the fatal argument with James. The Queen's Counsel representing James told the jury:

> Mrs Ramage was having her period, and you'll see in her handbag there were some tampons ... men tend to think that women get a bit scratchy at around that time—and if I'm wrong, dismiss it, okay? But Mrs Ramage went into that meeting, and according to Mr Ramage, what happened was that she said hurtful things.[61]

Writing two decades later, I still find these words, which outrageously were spoken in a 21st-century Australian courtroom, just as jarring as when I first heard them. In her book examining the death of Julie Ramage, Karen Kissane remarks on this moment in the trial:

> Let's face it: who was it who was really having a bad day emotionally? Who was it who lost his temper in a murderous rage? Not the partner wearing a tampon ... What is on trial here is not just Julie's sexual behaviour but female sexuality itself.[62]

Kissane is alluding to other evidence presented during the trial that sought to draw attention to the affairs Julie had had before and after her separation from her spouse and eventual killer. While James was presented as a successful businessman, a provider for his family, a husband grieving the breakdown of his marriage, Julie was painted as an unfaithful wife and a 'scratchy' woman.

At the end of the Ramage trial in the Victorian Supreme Court, the jury was invited to consider three possibilities: that James had murdered Julie; that he had acted without intent to kill and should be convicted of manslaughter; or that the prosecutors had failed to negate the partial defence of provocation and that he should be convicted of manslaughter on that ground. Ramage was subsequently convicted of manslaughter.

This was not justice. It is unacceptable for our criminal courts to be complicit in promulgating the idea that women bring about men's violence, that it is their responsibility and by extension their fault. When we blame women for men's violence, we utterly fail to hold men to account. Examples like this, where men kill women in the name of possession, are a sobering reminder of the patriarchal society that we continue to live in. Julie Ramage represents one well-known case among numerous other Australian women who have been killed by the men they dared to leave.

Since James Ramage's conviction for killing Julie, there has been significant reform across Australia of the partial defence of provocation, an archaic defence that serves to diminish the severity of the actions of *provoked* men.[63] Several states have abolished the partial defence entirety, while others have heavily restricted its application in a bid to ensure that it cannot be used in defence of the lethal actions of jealous men. And yet, despite this progress, I find it outrageous that women are still routinely judged and condemned for the violence committed against them. All too often, reactions to violence against women continue to focus on *how could she* as opposed to *how could he*. How could *she* let him do this? What did *she* do to cause that? The message is loud and clear: the women of Australia are responsible for the violence perpetrated against them by men.

STRANGER DANGER

It is absurd to think that even where women are killed by men unknown to them, such narratives of victim-blaming can persist.

'Stranger danger' is a popularised term that refers among other scenarios to the women's deaths that strike a unique fear in the community—the killing of women by men unknown to them. In the public imagination, it can be the stuff of thriller films spun out from the infamy of Jack the Ripper, the strange men who should be feared and avoided whenever possible, especially at night. It would be remiss of me to say that there is no threat from the unknown perpetrator in Australia, but

I can say that the risk an Australian woman faces from a stranger is significantly lower than the risk she faces from men she knows and trusts. The killing of women by a complete stranger or by someone whom they have just met accounts for 13 per cent of homicides in Australia.[64] It is a rare event. Still, when they do occur, these killings uniquely capture the public's attention, and the women's names become etched into the public vernacular: Jill Meagher, Eurydice Dixon, Masa Vukotic, Aiia Maasarwe—all Victorian incidents, each woman killed by a man unknown to her while walking home. The cases are unrelated and occurred years apart, but the names of these women have become inextricably linked because of the everyday activity they were each undertaking when attacked, and the horrific nature of their deaths.

While a statistical rarity, for women—indeed, for every Australian—this is nonetheless the stuff of nightmares. This was immediately apparent when, on a Sunday afternoon in April 2024, at Bondi Junction shopping centre in Sydney, forty-year-old Joel Cauchi murdered six people—including five women—and injured twelve others. Writing shortly after the incident, during which her daughter was at the shopping centre and was evacuated by police, author Kerri Sackville commented:

> It could have been me, but there is little comfort in my good fortune. Because it wasn't me, but it was six other

> people, five of them women, brutally murdered in plain sight. They were random women, women with families, women who were cherished and loved. They were women who would have felt perfectly safe, who should have run their errands and then made their way home.[65]

While there remain more questions than answers in relation to the Bondi killings, and no doubt inquiries to come will provide important insights into the actions and motivations of the killer, the horrific case provides another example of women's insecurity in the midst of a national crisis of men's violence against women.

However, that is not the only reason why I want to raise this topic here. I do so because when it comes to stranger danger, as with the violence that occurs within our homes, it is so often women who are assigned the responsibility to maintain their own safety. This was a key message in the comments made in 2015 by the head of the Victoria Police homicide squad, detective inspector Mick Hughes, following the daytime killing of seventeen-year-old Masa Vukotic in a Melbourne park by Shaun Price. Speaking on radio, Hughes offered this advice: 'I suggest to people, particularly females, [that] they shouldn't be alone in parks. I'm sorry to say that that is the case. We just need to be a little more careful, a little more security conscious.'[66]

This is an enormously troubling response, especially as it was delivered by a senior member of the police. Perpetrator accountability matters, but when we focus on the behaviour of the victim, we do so at the expense of holding the perpetrator to account. As a consequence, perpetrators can remain in the shadows in responses to men's violence against women. This is not what Australian women need. While improving victim-survivor safety should always be the priority, to achieve this there is a need to keep the spotlight on the perpetrator.

MEDIA REPORTING OF MALE VIOLENCE

One reason why victim-blaming narratives continue to proliferate, with limited accountability placed on the perpetrators of domestic, family and sexual violence, is that perpetrators can be all but invisible in media reports of men's violence against women. This is most problematic where the media is intent on describing the perpetrator in positive terms, such as by calling them a 'good father' or a 'hard worker'—labelling that merely supports a responsibility-minimising narrative whereby the man's lethal actions were completely out of character, seemingly occurring out of the blue.

Writing in *British Vogue* in July 2024, a week after the horrific killings in Hertfordshire of Carol, Hannah and Louise Hunt, allegedly by Louise's ex-partner Kyle Clifford, Janey Starling called out poor media reporting of the case:

> When a man is arrested on suspicion of murdering three women and media headlines describe him as a 'nice, normal guy', it's clear our society has a serious problem … The press has a habit of branding dangerous men as 'nice guys', which negates their accountability. The 'nice guy' narrative, usually built from quotes from neighbours in the immediate aftermath of a death, insults victims and damages public understanding of domestic abuse. It reinforces the lie that men who murder women do it spontaneously because something has pushed them to do so. In the same vein, we see violent men reduced to 'jilted' or 'scorned lovers', which indirectly holds victims responsible for men's lethal violence.[67]

This is not an observation specific to the United Kingdom. In Australia over the last year, we have continued to see irresponsible examples of media coverage that serve to promote a positive view of a perpetrator and in turn reduce public perceptions of their culpability and harm. Take, for example, Australian media coverage in the fortnight following the brutal October 2023 killing of 21-year-old Lilie James, allegedly by her 24-year-old ex-boyfriend Paul Thijssen. This coverage incessantly focused on the private school role held by Thijssen, while a school-wide newsletter sent by the head of his former school in the days following the killing described him as 'an absolute delight' and 'not a monster'.[68]

At a time when serious efforts are being made to inform community understandings of domestic, family and sexual violence, and to combat the myths that surround such abuse, such media narratives and public statements can be extremely harmful.

THE NEED FOR PREVENTION AND PROGRESS

So far, I have largely focused on what we know about abuse, and what happens *after* violence is perpetrated, but let's take a step back to understand why an emphasis on prevention is absolutely critical to addressing our national crisis of men's violence against women.

The drivers of men's violence against women in Australia are gender inequality and other forms of oppression. Australia's national prevention organisation, Our Watch, has led the development of *Change the Story*, a national framework to inform the prevention of violence against women.[69] *Change the Story* highlights the centrality of gender inequality to this violence, and the need for cultural, structural and systemic changes across society to address it. Former senator and current member of the United Nations Committee on the Elimination of Discrimination against Women, Natasha Stott Despoja, has explained: 'Violence emerges in a broader social construct. This is a society where the underlying conditions of gender inequality mean that violence is often condoned, trivialised or considered a private matter.'[70]

If we are to advance gender equality in Australia, we need to acknowledge and address where inequalities exist, beginning with an admission that gender inequality is heavily present in the Australian community. Former Australian sex discrimination commissioner Kate Jenkins has described gender inequality as Australia's 'dirty secret'.[71] We know that it is present throughout our workplaces and our communities, and we know that it is one of the key drivers of violence against women. Inequalities must be named, identified and remedied. We cannot solve a problem that we feel too uncomfortable—or too paralysed by the status quo—to call out.

In her speech at the 2021 March4Justice in Canberra, victim-survivor advocate Saxon Mullins was clear on how to tackle gender inequality, with her call to action targeting the men of Australia:

> One in five women have experienced sexual violence. Men, where do you think these perpetrators are hiding? They are your friends. They are your co-workers. They are your football mates, and they are your friends from school. It is not enough to say, 'I would never rape someone.' You would need to think about your behaviours. Do you look the other way when your mate yells at his girlfriend on a night out? Do you complain that people are too sensitive when someone calls out 'you're racist' or 'you're transphobic' remarks? If any of this rings a bell, I remind you, you do not need to

> imagine that you know someone who perpetrates such an act. Because you don't just know them, you helped them, you helped to create a toxic culture of … misogyny and transphobia and racism that has allowed them to thrive.[72]

Alongside Saxon's call to action, one of the most powerful reflections I have heard on what drives men's violence came from an unexpected source. In 2014, Tom Meagher, whose wife Jill Meagher was murdered in Melbourne in September 2012 by serial rapist and now convicted murderer Adrian Bayley, wrote an article reflecting on the moment he heard Bayley speak in court:

> I had formed an image that this man was not human, that he existed as a singular force of pure evil who somehow emerged from the ether. Something about his ability to weave together nouns, verbs and pronouns to form real, intelligible sentences forced a re-focus, one that required a look at the spectrum of men's violence against women, and its relation to Bayley and the society from which he came. By insulating myself with the intellectually evasive dismissal of violent men as psychotic or sociopathic aberrations, I self-comforted by avoiding the more terrifying concept that violent men are socialised by the ingrained sexism and entrenched masculinity that permeates everything from our daily interactions all the way up to our highest institutions.[73]

For me, Tom Meagher eloquently confronted the reality that gender inequality and the associated disrespect towards women in our community underpin the violent actions of men such as Bayley. I was fortunate to spend some time with Tom at a conference in the beautiful Irish city of Cork nearly ten years ago now, after he had moved back to Ireland and was working in the violence-against-women sector. Tom's presentation at that conference encouraged a better understanding of the problematic cultures within our society that allow men's violence to thrive, and the preventive work needed to address this crisis.

We simply won't achieve the substantive prevention of men's violence against women without significant progress towards the achievement of gender equality. A failure to do so will guarantee that in the years to come, we will continue to count women's deaths on a weekly basis.

I admit that at times I worry that 'gender inequality' is a term that can be thrown around and so mistaken for a vague concept or an abstract one. But make no mistake—it is real. We can point to it in the everyday experiences of women and girls across Australia. The Australian Workplace Gender Equality Agency reports that as of January 2024, the gender pay gap nationally stands at just over 21 per cent. In this context, gender inequality refers to the extra hours, days or indeed weeks that a woman is required to work to earn the same salary as a male counterpart. It is the fact that in Australia, women make up over 50 per cent of the workforce but less than 20 per cent of CEOs and board chairs.[74]

Gender inequality is the fact that women in Australia retire with significantly less superannuation than men and consequently are at higher risk of living in poverty or facing homelessness in their later years.

HOW DO WE COMPARE ON GENDER EQUALITY AGAINST OTHER COUNTRIES?

Every year, the World Economic Forum provides global analyses of what is termed the 'gender gap'. The most recent analysis shows that at the current rate of progress, it is likely to take 134 years to reach gender parity worldwide.[75] My daughter is seven years old and, on this calculation, neither she nor her children are likely to live their lives in a gender-equal world. That is such a depressing thought. But it gets more confronting. The outlook in Australia may be even worse than the global average according to some measures.

In 2006, Australia was ranked fifteenth in the world for gender parity. Not exactly a leader in the space, but perhaps borderline respectable. Fifteen years later, Australia's performance in addressing the gender gap declined and our position globally became neither leading nor respectable. As of early 2021, taking into account the four measures of economic participation and opportunity, political empowerment, educational attainment, health and survival, Australia ranked fiftieth in the world on the gender gap.

By contrast, the Nordic nations of Iceland, Finland and Norway took the top three rankings, followed by our closest neighbour, New Zealand. The United Kingdom sat in twenty-third place. And in the immediate aftermath of Donald Trump's presidency, a four-year term during which concerns surrounding the erosion of women's rights were front and centre, the United States appeared in thirtieth spot—twenty countries above Australia.

When you break down Australia's ranking in 2021 against each of those four measures, the results are even more sobering. Australia's performance on economic participation and opportunity was ranked lower than its overall average—in seventieth position globally. In regard to political empowerment, we were ranked fifty-fourth. Our ranking on health and survival—ninety-ninth—was the most telling, however. This measure takes into account the early death of women due to violence as well as disease, malnutrition and other factors. Australia's ranking is perhaps unsurprising given that intimate partner violence contributes more to the disease burden in Australia than any other risk factor in women aged 18–44 years, more than well-known risk factors such as tobacco use, high cholesterol or use of illicit drugs.

There has been some progress since then. Findings from the World Economic Forum released in June

2023 showed that Australia had lifted its position to twenty-sixth in the world on the gender gap. Australia's results on economic participation shifted it into thirty-eighth spot, and for health and survival there was a small increase in its ranking to eighty-ninth—hardly a point of celebration, but progress nonetheless.

However, our progress was not linear. On educational attainment we fell significantly. In 2021, Australia shared first place for educational attainment with twenty-six other countries—two years later, we ranked seventy-eighth. It is frightening to see how quickly progress can be lost.

These findings show us that while Australia has a legacy of having some of the most educated women in the world, those same highly educated women still experience inequality in many facets of their lives. And they are being killed at the rate of, on average, at least one each week, and victimised by men's violence in all facets of their lives—be it the home, the workplace or in public.

SO, WHAT CAN I DO?

This is a question I am often asked—by family members and friends, by value-aligned workplaces, and in conversations at community events. The short answer is that everyone has a role to play. We can all meaningfully be part of efforts in Australia to address men's violence against women and children.

As an individual, figuring out how to make a difference in this space can feel overwhelming or intimidating. But small acts can go far. Research tells us that sexism and disrespect towards women contribute to a culture that allows, justifies and can even promote violence towards women. That makes challenging disrespect towards women everyone's responsibility. So when a friend, family member or work colleague makes a disrespectful remark, joke or comment, call it out. This doesn't have to be done confrontationally—small nudges can make a difference over time.

This is all part of the work needed to drive attitudinal and social change. And change absolutely is possible. For examples, look no further than the recent successes of Australia's national football team, the Matildas, and the AFL Women's league, which have changed the national conversation on women in sport and equality across sporting codes. Because of them, you will hopefully never hear the words 'You kick like a girl' or 'You throw like a girl' levelled as a criticism anymore.

Small acts of support can also be transformational for victim-survivors. For many women and children experiencing violence, it is their family, friends, neighbours or co-workers who may first become aware of their victimisation. Bystanders represent an early point of possible intervention, and critically, an early opportunity to connect victims with the relevant support services and engage in safety planning. Unfortunately, family and friends often do not know what to say or do, and are paralysed by that uncertainty into saying or doing nothing.

The potential consequences of inaction among bystanders can be significant. This was illustrated in April 2020 in the killing of Kim Murphy in her Adelaide home, allegedly by her former male partner. Occurring in the midst of the introduction of public health lockdowns due to COVID-19, the case struck me as a terrifying example of the violence that could take place out of sight during the pandemic. Initial investigations following Kim's death revealed that, the night before she was killed, several neighbours had heard disturbances at the property, including a threat to kill, and the mother crying for help. But no-one called the police.

The investigating police officer on the case, detective superintendent Des Bray, said:

> It is a sad reflection on society that people would hear that and not ring the police. I'm at a complete loss to understand why anybody wouldn't do something and go to the aid or ensure that somebody went to the aid of a woman who was screaming for help.[76]

The killing of Kim Murphy and the comments from Bray underline the critical role of onlookers, including the potential for well-informed bystander interventions, in saving the lives of Australian women and preventing future acts of violence. To date, very little attention has been paid to this space in Australia beyond advertising campaigns.

If there is one message I would like you to take from reading this book, it is this: if someone discloses their experience of abuse to you, it is absolutely OK to feel nervous as to how that conversation will play out. You are not expected to suddenly become a specialist family violence counsellor, nor is it your personal responsibility to keep that individual safe. But you can say 'I believe you' and 'I'm sorry this has happened to you'. You may be the first person that individual has ever told, and just confirming that they have been believed is incredibly powerful.

THE ROLE OF WORKPLACES

There is also a key role for workplaces across Australia to play. Indeed, in recent years workplaces have been identified as one of the key sites for change, both in terms of progressing gender equality and supporting victims of domestic and family violence. So why do workplaces matter? Men and women spend a significant amount of their daily time in the workplace, so it can be heavily influenced by men's violence against women, and in turn heavily influential as a location for improving victim-survivor safety.

Research shows that domestic and family violence can take victim-survivors out of the workforce, it can impact the degree of their contribution when in the workforce, and it can prevent victim-survivors from entering the workforce. A report by the Champions of Change Coalition found that 62 per cent of women who have experienced, or who are currently experiencing, domestic and family violence are in the paid workforce, and that nearly 50 per cent of women who disclosed that they had experienced domestic and family violence reported that it affected their capacity to get to work.[77] Of these women, nearly one in five reported that the domestic violence followed them into the workplace; for example, in the form of abusive calls or emails, or their partner physically coming to the workplace.

In 2022, I was involved in a study at Monash which involved a survey of 3000 Australian victim-survivors of domestic and family violence who were employed in an Australian workplace at the time of their victimisation.[78] Four in five victims surveyed reported that their job was impacted by their experience of violence. This included negative impacts on career progression, ability to concentrate at work, productivity, job enjoyment, and punctuality. Survey respondents additionally reported that their experience of domestic and family violence also impacted their relationship with work colleagues, leading to them socially withdrawing from their co-workers.

Compared to a decade ago we have significantly better research-based understandings of the impact of abuse on work performance. It is critical that these insights are utilised to inform workplace support practice and policies, ensuring that victim-survivors are not subjected to performance management or put at risk of demotion or employment termination in the midst of abuse.

Looking to perpetrators, global studies have found that up to 78 per cent of people who perpetrate domestic and family violence have done so during work hours using workplace resources. This is often referred to as 'workplace interference strategies', and our survey found that one in two victim-survivors had experienced this form of abuse. The impacts were immediate and wide-ranging. One victim-survivor described in our survey how, 'By contacting me constantly at work I felt on edge and constant checking my phone which cause[d] prob[lems] in my performance.'

Impeding access to employment and performance at work was used as a key tactic by perpetrators to disrupt employment stability for the victim. Our research really drove home for me the need to ensure that our national and state-based responses recognise that the workplace and the perpetration of domestic, family and sexual violence in intimate partner relationships are not inseparable. Our policies, both within and beyond the workplace, must reflect this if we are to uphold a victim-centred approach.

We can put a cost on these workplace impacts. In Australia, it is estimated that violence against women costs

$26 billion annually.[79] Of this, $1.9 billion is attributed directly to business and productivity losses, with perpetrator absenteeism costing $443 million, victim-survivor absenteeism costing $860 million, and additional management costs of $96 million. Looking specifically at workplace sexual harassment, it has been estimated that this form of violence alone costs the Australian economy $3.5 billion annually,[80] with $2.6 billion accorded to the lost productivity that occurs as a result;[81] this includes the toll of absenteeism as well as that of increased staff turnover and pressure on managerial time.

Instead of just incurring the costs of this violence, workplaces can make a real difference in addressing violence from the outset, and helping to prevent it.

For a victim-survivor, the availability of workplace supports—including policies like the now nationally legislated paid family violence leave—can mean the difference between choosing to stay in an abusive relationship due to financial insecurity, and having the independence to safely leave an abusive relationship and to be supported to maintain employment while navigating that decision.

At the early intervention level, workplaces also have an opportunity to raise awareness of what constitutes a healthy and respectful relationship. Importantly, workplaces can promote a culture where all violence, including coercive and controlling behaviours, are understood as unacceptable. Immunity from consequences and a lack of accountability for the use of violence in one setting will follow individuals into another setting. This has significant consequences for victims and for perpetrators.

I am hopeful that we are on the cusp of a significant increase in the attention paid to addressing violence in all its forms across Australian workplaces. In recent years I have observed the introduction of world-leading reforms that will propel this goal in workplaces, acting as a much-needed legislative stick. For example, the federal government has introduced access to ten days of paid domestic and family violence leave for all Australian employees, including casuals. We also now have the world-leading Respect@Work legislation, which imposes a positive obligation on Australian workplaces to prevent workplace sexual harassment.

These legislative changes are a critical piece of the domestic and family violence puzzle, but we also must do the trickier work of changing culture. It is imperative that we normalise help-seeking within the workplace, allowing individuals to feel comfortable and fully supported in doing so.

ACTION IS NEEDED FOR CHILDREN AND YOUNG PEOPLE

While in recent months across Australia we have seen, perhaps more so than ever before, continued media coverage of, and political attention paid to, men's violence against women, nowhere in the subsequent political announcements and promises have children as victim-survivors in their own right been considered. They have remained invisible, without a voice. Yet we know that they are devastatingly impacted by the crisis of men's violence, and that the goal of ending gender-based violence in one generation—as stated in the federal government's own *National Plan to End Violence against Women and Children, 2022–2032*—necessitates a focus on children and young people.

Let me be clear—ending gender-based violence within this generation requires a transformational focus on delivering improved outcomes for the next generation. If we are serious about eliminating violence against women, we need to stop the violence inflicted on children and comprehensively support their safety and recovery needs. This requires the development and integration of a trauma-informed and age-appropriate whole-of-system response, including services and initiatives throughout early childhood and school-based education settings, specialist domestic violence and family welfare service providers, child and young person mental health services, and youth justice.

Critically, there is a need to address the complete lack of appropriate housing options for children and young people experiencing and escaping domestic and family violence. Across Australia there are minimal domestic and family violence specialist crisis intervention and accommodation services designed for young people as victim-survivors in their own right. Young people escaping domestic and family violence in Australia presently face a significant risk of homelessness.[82]

While simple to list, these actions will require substantive political will and long-term government funding if we are to effectively meet the needs of Australian children and young people impacted by domestic, family and sexual violence. To date, this much-needed political will has not been forthcoming. Indeed, two years into the national plan's timeframe, it is unclear what actions have been taken—if any—to realise this acknowledgement of policy and practice. What child-centred service supports have been put in place in each state and territory to meet the safety needs of children escaping violence? What crisis housing services for children and young people have been delivered to ensure children are not choosing between a violent home and homelessness? And critically, where is the much-needed expansion of recovery and healing services for children and young people?

It is not enough for children to merely survive a childhood of violence. Surely the aim is for all Australian children to thrive.

THE ELIMINATION OF VIOLENCE

Globally, we are experiencing an alarming moment in history, with threats to women's rights emerging in many settings: the destructive winding back of women's rights in Afghanistan, the rise of dangerous manosphere influencers such as Andrew Tate (who at the time of writing is awaiting trial in Romania on charges including human trafficking), the recent overturning of the US Supreme Court's decision in *Roe v. Wade*,[83] alongside many others. Australia is not immune from this global movement backwards—it would be naive to think we are. We must work very hard to ensure that gains in gender equality, and improvements in attitudes and respectful beliefs, are maintained, as we know that the consequences for women and children's safety will be significant if they aren't.

This means, as I hope I have imparted to you throughout this book, that we need to take women and children's safety seriously in all of the settings in which we live, work, learn and play. This must be prioritised in the same way as other issues that impact our national security.

Beyond the moral argument for doing so—which I would argue is enough—it also makes sense economically to invest in women's safety. At the community level, the price of men's violence against women is staggering. As noted earlier, violence against women and their children costs the Australian economy $26 billion every year. Almost 50 per cent of this—$10.4 billion—is attributed to the costs borne by victim-survivors, reflecting how they are at increased risk of chronic illness and pain, and reproductive health problems. While we have seen unprecedented federal funding directed at addressing violence against women in recent years, when we compare the costs that the community bears as a result of violence against women with the funding dedicated at the federal level to address this wicked problem, the imbalance is mind-boggling.

This disparity between the cost of the problem and the federal funding committed to addressing it, is not an anomaly. Nearly ten years ago now, in 2016, some colleagues from Monash University and I wrote an article for *The Age* calling out the higher priority given in the federal budget to terrorism as compared with violence against women.[84] In that year's budget, the government allocated $100 million over three years to domestic and family violence–related items, whereas $30 billion was directed to national security with the promise of 'keeping Australians safe' from terrorism threats abroad.[85] Of course, countering threats to national security must be a priority for the federal government, but the disparity in funding is unexplainable and inexcusable. In any given year over the last decade, more than twice as many women have been killed by their male intimate partners (current and former) than people killed in Australia as a result of terrorism offences since 2001. More recent comparisons have been made between the $368 billion allocated by the federal government to new submarines, and the $3.4 billion allocated to support women's safety and the work of the *National Plan to End Violence against Women and Children, 2022–2032.*

The funding committed to addressing violence against women and children needs to be commensurate with the gravity of the problem, but this is yet to happen. It would require the funding of a range of housing and accommodation options, so that women and children do not have to balance the threat of homelessness against the threat of staying with a violent partner/father. It would necessitate funding for specialist services to ensure that calls for help and for referral pathways do not go unanswered due to a lack of resources. And of course, we must fund prevention, including education and community-led programs, or we will still be having this conversation in ten or twenty years' time.

We also need leadership that commits heart, mind and wallet to securing the safety of all persons by meaningfully progressing the elimination of violence against women and children. Such transformative leadership requires the creation of genuine partnerships with the community, experts in the field, and importantly, victim-survivor advocates. National efforts must bring together diverse views and forge a commitment to true co-design—privileging lived experience, frontline expertise and community-specific understanding in the design and development of systems, policies and practices.

I am extremely conscious of the fact that this book speaks largely about white women's experiences of male intimate partner violence, and men's violence against children. While there are nods to diverse experiences where possible, I do not purport to talk about, or for, communities to which I do not belong or with whom I have not consulted in depth. Their voices are far more powerful than mine, and in acknowledging the shortcomings of my own intervention, I implore those with the platforms and leadership to do so to find ways to elevate diverse women and children's views on, and experiences of, domestic, family and sexual violence.

Finally, while ambitious, and feeling far from achievable after the horror of the first six months of 2024, the elimination of all forms of violence against women and children must be the end goal. I refuse to give up on the potential for absolute change and a safer Australian community. The extent of men's violence against women and children in Australia is a national crisis, and our inaction to date in responding to it in all its forms is our national shame. We must act now to change this—all of us.

ACKNOWLEDGEMENTS

In the midst of the ongoing national crisis of violence against women and children, I am very grateful to Greg Bain for encouraging me to write this book. Recognising the mission of the In the National Interest series to foster informed discussions on matters of national importance, I am honoured to address such a critical issue as part of this series.

It has been wonderful to work with Paul Smitz again. Paul, thank you for your meticulous editing and collaborative spirit, which have been invaluable in shaping this book into what I envisioned.

Over the past decade, I have had the privilege of engaging with numerous academics, policymakers, practitioners, advocates and victim-survivors, both in Australia and internationally. These interactions have greatly enriched my work, and I am profoundly grateful to be part of a broader movement dedicated to ending violence against women and children.

This book is dedicated to my three children—Matilda, William and Edward—and to my husband, Michael. They are the vibrant, inspiring and absolutely brilliant centre of my world. Thank you for your unwavering support for everything I do.

NOTES

1 C Read, 'Accused Murderer's Phone Recordings Could Be Key to Wife's Tractor Slasher Death', *The Brisbane Times*, 16 February 2024.

2 M Bali and S Patidar, 'Father of Chaithanya Madhagani Claims Son-in-Law Ashok Raj Varikuppala Revealed Location of Wife's Body to Police', *ABC News*, 14 March 2024.

3 As cited in R Willingham and R Kirkham, 'Alleged Murder of 23-Year-Old Hannah McGuire Reignites Calls to Prevent Violence against Women', *ABC News*, 9 April 2024.

4 R Peppiatt and Nine News Perth, 'Man Charged with Murdering Warnbro Mother Erica Hay', *The Age*, 28 April 2024.

5 K Fitz-Gibbon and S Meyer, 'What We Can All Do to Stop Death Toll of Women Climbing', *The Canberra Times*, 3 November 2023.

6 J Gilmore, 'Six Women Killed in Five Days, You Need to Engage with This Crisis', *The Sydney Morning Herald*, 9 October 2018.

7 As listed in R Batty and K Fitz-Gibbon, 'The Case for a Federal Minister for Children', *The Saturday Paper*, 29 June 2024.
8 T Rose, 'Deaths of Three Children in Lalor Park House Fire Leaves NSW with "Deep Wound", Premier Says', *The Guardian*, 9 July 2024.
9 United Nations Office on Drugs and Crime, *Killing of Women and Girls By Their Intimate Partner or Other Family Members*, Data Matters, 3 November 2021.
10 Australian Bureau of Statistics, 'Personal Safety, Australia', 2023, https://www.abs.gov.au/statistics/people/crime-and-justice/personal-safety-australia/latest-release (viewed July 2024).
11 Ibid.
12 C Blumer, 'Australian Police Deal with Domestic Violence Every Two Minutes', *ABC News*, 21 April 2016.
13 Australian Bureau of Statistics, 'Personal Safety, Australia', 2023, https://www.abs.gov.au/statistics/people/crime-and-justice/personal-safety-australia/latest-release (viewed July 2024).
14 Ibid.
15 National Domestic and Family Violence Bench Book, 'Economic and Financial Abuse—Context Statement', 2023, https://dfvbenchbook.aija.org.au/understanding-domestic-and-family-violence/economic-abuse (viewed July 2024).
16 Department of Social Services, *National Plan to End Violence against Women and Children, 2022–2032*, Commonwealth Government of Australia, Canberra, 2022.
17 B Mathews et al., 'The Prevalence of Child Maltreatment in Australia: Findings from a National Survey', *Medical*

Journal of Australia, vol. 218, suppl. 6, 2023, S13–S18; D Lawrence et al., 'The Association between Child Maltreatment and Health Risk Behaviours and Conditions throughout Life in the Australian Child Maltreatment Study', *Medical Journal of Australia*, vol. 218, suppl. 6, 2023, S34–S39.

18 Ibid.

19 *R v Freeman* [2011] VSC 139, per Coghlan J at 55.

20 Australian Domestic and Family Violence Death Review Network, and Australia's National Research Organisation for Women's Safety (ANROWS), *Filicides in a Domestic and Family Violence Context 2010–2018*, ANROWS, Sydney, 2024.

21 Australian Bureau of Statistics, 'National Aboriginal and Torres Strait Islander Social Survey, 2014–2015', cat. no. 4714.0, *2016*, https://www.abs.gov.au/ausstats/abs@.nsf/mf/4714.0 (viewed July 2024).

22 Yoorrook Justice Commission, 'Transcript of Day 10—Public Hearing', pp. 35–45.

23 S-A Hunter, 'Aboriginal Women Have Fought against Gendered Violence Perpetrated By White Men Since Day One', *Women's Agenda*, March 2021.

24 Human Rights Law Centre and Change the Record, *Over-Represented and Overlooked: the Crisis of Aboriginal and Torres Strait Islander Women's Growing Over-Imprisonment*, 2017.

25 N Pfitzner et al., *When 'Stay at Home' Isn't Safe: Domestic and Family Violence and the Coronavirus Pandemic*, Palgrave Pivot, Palgrave, UK, 2023.

26 N Pfitzner, K Fitz-Gibbon and J True, 'When Staying Home Isn't Safe: Australian Practitioner Experiences of Responding to Intimate Partner Violence during

COVID-19 Restrictions', *Journal of Gender Based Violence*, 2022, p. 6.

27 K Fitz-Gibbon et al., *Disconnected & Insecure: the Intersection between Experiences of Long COVID and Intimate Partner Violence*, Monash University, Clayton, Vic., 2024.

28 JS Chandan et al., 'Intimate Partner Violence and the Risk of Developing Fibromyalgia and Chronic Fatigue Syndrome', *Journal of Interpersonal Violence*, vol. 36, nos 21–22, 2021, NP12279–NP12298.

29 Australian Institute of Health and Welfare, *Long COVID in Australia: A Review of the Literature*, 2022.

30 K Fitz-Gibbon et al., *Disconnected & Insecure: the Intersection between Experiences of Long COVID and Intimate Partner Violence*, Monash University, Clayton, Vic., 2024, p. 22.

31 Australian Bureau of Statistics (ABS), *Disability and Violence—in Focus: Crime and Justice Statistics*, ABS, Canberra, 2021; People with Disability Australia (PWDA), and Domestic Violence NSW (DVNSW), *Women with Disability and Domestic and Family Violence: a Guide for Policy and Practice*, PWDA & DVNSW, NSW, 2021.

32 T Mitra-Kahn, C Newbigin and S Hardefeldt, 'Invisible Women, Invisible Violence: Understanding and Improving Data on the Experiences of Domestic and Family Violence and Sexual Assault for Diverse Groups of Women: State of Knowledge Paper', *ANROWS Landscapes*, DD01, 2016; K Thurber et al., 'Risk of Severe Illness from COVID-19 among Aboriginal and Torres Strait Islander Adults: the Construct of "Vulnerable Populations" Obscures the Root Cause of Health Inequities', *Indigenous Health*, vol. 45, no. 6, 2021, pp. 658–63.

33 World Health Organization, 'Violence against Women', *Fact Sheet*, 25 March 2024.

34 M Tiemensma et al., 'Chronic Traumatic Encephalopathy (CTE) in the Context of Longstanding Intimate Partner Violence', *Acta Neuropathol*, vol. 148, article no. 1.

35 Department of Social Services, *National Plan to End Violence against Women and Children, 2022–2032*, Commonwealth Government of Australia, Canberra, 2022.

36 K Fitz-Gibbon et al., *Adolescent Family Violence in Australia: A National Study of Prevalence, History of Childhood Victimisation and Impacts*, Research Report issue 15, Australia's National Research Organisation for Women's Safety, September 2022.

37 Ibid.

38 E Stark, *Coercive Control: the Entrapment of Women in Personal Life*, Oxford University Press, New York, 2009.

39 H Boxall and A Morgan, *Experiences of Coercive Control among Australian Women*, Statistical Bulletin no. 30, Australian Institute of Criminology, Canberra, 2021.

40 NSW Domestic Violence Death Review Team, *Domestic Violence Death Review Team Report 2015–2017*, Sydney, 2020.

41 L Twyford, 'Coercive Control a Factor in almost Every Domestic Violence Death Reviewed in Canberra over Two Decades', *ABC News*, 4 March 2024.

42 H Gleeson, 'Hannah Clarke "Did Everything" She Could to Protect Herself and Her Children. Experts Explain Why It Wasn't Enough', *ABC News*, 10 March 2020.

43 R Riga, 'Hannah Clarke's Parents Push for Coercive Control to Be Made a Crime One Year on from Horrific Murders', *ABC News*, 14 February 2021.

44 Coroners Court of Queensland, *Findings of Inquest: Inquest into the Deaths of Hannah Ashlie Clarke, Aaliyah Anne Baxter, Laianah Grace Baxter, Trey Rowan Charles Baxter, and Rowan Charles Baxter*, file nos 2020/741, 2020/739, 2020/740, 2020/738 & 2020/736, delivered 29 June 2022, Southport, Qld; findings by Jane Bentley, Deputy State Coroner, at pp. 37–62.

45 M King, '"Intimate Terrorism": Why the Murders of Hannah, Aaliyah, Laianah and Trey Must Spark Change', *The Sydney Morning Herald*, 20 November 2020.

46 K Fitz-Gibbon et al., *Securing Women's Lives: Examining System Interactions and Perpetrator Risk in Intimate Femicide Sentencing Judgments over a Decade in Australia*, Monash University and University of Liverpool, 2024.

47 M Perkins, 'Thompson, Stabbed to Death by Ex-Partner: Coroner', *The Age*, 21 April 2016.

48 Coroners Court of Victoria, *Inquest into the Death of Kelly Ann Thompson*, file no. COR 2014 000824, 2014.

49 Ibid.

50 Royal Commission into Family Violence, *Report and Recommendations*, Victoria, 2016.

51 ACT Children and Young People Commissioner, *Now You Have Heard Us, What Will You Do?: Insights from Young People on Domestic and Family Violence*, ACT Human Rights Commission, Canberra, 2021.

52 I Gray, *Finding—Inquest into the Death of Luke Geoffrey Batty*, Coroners Court of Victoria, Melbourne, 2015.

53 M McKenzie, 'Rosie Batty: the Private Toll of Public Grief', *The Saturday Paper*, 31 March 2019.

54 Rosie Batty, *Hope*, HarperCollins, Sydney, 2024.

55 D Anderson and D Saunders, 'Leaving an Abusive Partner: An Empirical Review of Predictors, the Process of

Leaving, and Psychological Well-Being', *Trauma, Violence & Abuse*, vol. 4, no. 2, 2003, p. 171.

56 *R v Ramage* [2004] VSC 508, per Osborn J at 22.

57 Ibid., at 33.

58 Ibid., at 63.

59 Ibid., at 10.

60 Ibid., at 46.

61 K Kissane, *Silent Death: the Killing of Julie Ramage*, Hodder, Sydney, 2004, p. 184.

62 Ibid.

63 On this, see further K Fitz-Gibbon, *Homicide Law Reform, Gender and the Provocation Defence: A Comparative Perspective*, Palgrave MacMillan, Hampshire, 2014.

64 H Miles and S Bricknell, *Homicide in Australia: 2022–23*, Statistical Report no. 46, Australian Institute of Criminology, Canberra, 2024.

65 K Sackville, 'This Was a Safe Space for All Women. Now It's Been Shattered', *The Sydney Morning Herald*, 14 April 2024.

66 M Davey, 'Masa Vukotic Had the Right to Be in a Park Alone. Victoria Police Must Apologise for Saying She Didn't', *The Guardian*, 20 March 2015.

67 J Starling, 'Stop Calling Suspected Killers "Nice Guys": the Media Has to Do Better in Its Reporting of Violence against Women', *British Vogue*, 12 July 2024.

68 G Stonehouse and D Kozaki, 'Shore School Headmaster Criticised for Comments about Lilie James's Suspected Murderer in Newsletter', *ABC News*, 4 November 2023.

69 Our Watch, *Change the Story: A Shared Framework for the Primary Prevention of Violence against Women in Australia*, 2nd edn, 2021.

70 Natasha Stott Despoja, 'Australia's Ongoing National Emergency—Violence against Women', address to the National Press Club, Canberra, 19 August 2020.

71 K Jenkins, 'Accelerating Change: Gender Equality from the Household to the Workplace', address to the National Press Club, Canberra, 20 April 2016.

72 R Dexter, '"Men, Where Do You Think These Perpetrators Are Hiding?" Saxon Mullins Calls for Change', *The Sydney Morning Herald*, 15 March 2021.

73 T Meagher, 'The Danger of the Monster Myth', *ABC News*, 18 April 2014.

74 J Lim, 'Why Chief Executive Women Is Calling for 40:40:20 Targets', *Melbourne Business School News*, 6 March 2024.

75 World Economic Forum, *Global Gender Gap: Insight Report*, June 2024.

76 B Siebert, 'Man Charged with Murder after Woman's Body Found at Morphett Vale House', *ABC News*, 17 April 2020.

77 Champions of Change Coalition, *Playing Our Part: A Framework for Workplace Action on Domestic and Family Violence*, 2021.

78 E McNicol, K Fitz-Gibbon and S Brewer, *From Workplace Sabotage to Embedded Supports: Examining the Impact of Domestic and Family Violence across Australian Workplaces*, Monash University, Clayton, Vic., 2022.

79 Australian Government, *Women's Economic Security Statement 2020*, Canberra, 2020, p. 62.

80 Ibid.

81 Deloitte, *The Economic Costs of Sexual Harassment in the Workplace: Final Report*, Canberra, 2019.

82 See also T Corrie and S Moore, *AMPLIFY: Turning up the Volume on Young People and Family Violence*, Melbourne City Mission, 2021; S Convery, '"Young People Are

Invisible": Family Violence Survivors Falling through Cracks at Crisis Services', *The Guardian*, 3 July 2022.

83 R Sifris, 'Now that Roe v Wade Has Been Overturned, What Are the Consequences?', *Monash Lens*, 27 June 2022.

84 K Fitz-Gibbon, J McCulloch and J Maher, 'Little in Budget to Counter Family Violence', *The Age*, 4 May 2016.

85 Commonwealth of Australia, *Budget 2016–17 Overview*, 3 May 2016.

IN THE NATIONAL INTEREST

Other books on the issues that matter:

David Anderson *Now More than Ever: Australia's ABC*
Kevin Bell *Housing: The Great Australian Right*
Bill Bowtell *Unmasked: The Politics of Pandemics*
Michael Bradley *System Failure: The Silencing of Rape Survivors*
Melissa Castan & Lynette Russell *Time to Listen: An Indigenous Voice to Parliament*
Inala Cooper *Marrul: Aboriginal Identity & the Fight for Rights*
Kim Cornish *The Post-Pandemic Child*
Samantha Crompvoets *Blood Lust, Trust & Blame*
Satyajit Das *Fortune's Fool: Australia's Choices*
Richard Denniss *Big: The Role of the State in the Modern Economy*
Rachel Doyle *Power & Consent*
Jo Dyer *Burning Down the House: Reconstructing Modern Politics*
Wayne Errington & Peter van Onselen *Who Dares Loses: Pariah Policies*
Gareth Evans *Good International Citizenship: The Case for Decency*
Paul Farrell *Gladys: A Leader's Undoing*
Kate Fitz-Gibbon *Our National Shame: Violence against Women*
Paul Fletcher *Governing in the Internet Age*
Carrillo Gantner *Dismal Diplomacy, Disposable Sovereignty: Our Problem with China & America*
Quentin Grafton *Retelling Australia's Water Story*
Jill Hennessy *Respect*
Lucinda Holdforth *21st-Century Virtues: How They Are Failing Our Democracy*

(continued from previous page)

Simon Holmes à Court *The Big Teal*
Andrew Jaspan & Lachlan Guselli *The Consultancy Conundrum: The Hollowing Out of the Public Sector*
Andrew Leigh *Fair Game: Lessons from Sport for a Fairer Society & a Stronger Economy*
Ian Lowe *Australia on the Brink: Avoiding Environmental Ruin*
John Lyons *Dateline Jerusalem: Journalism's Toughest Assignment*
Richard Marles *Tides that Bind: Australia in the Pacific*
Fiona McLeod *Easy Lies & Influence*
Michael Mintrom *Advancing Human Rights*
Louise Newman *Rape Culture*
Martin Parkinson *A Decade of Drift*
Jennifer Rayner *Climate Clangers: The Bad Ideas Blocking Real Action*
Isabelle Reinecke *Courting Power: Law, Democracy & the Public Interest in Australia*
Abul Rizvi *Population Shock*
Kevin Rudd *The Case for Courage*
Don Russell *Leadership*
Scott Ryan *Challenging Politics*
Ronli Sifris *Towards Reproductive Justice*
Kate Thwaites & Jenny Macklin *Enough Is Enough*
Simon Wilkie *The Digital Revolution: A Survival Guide*
Carla Wilshire *Time to Reboot: Feminism in the Algorithm Age*
Campbell Wilson *Living with AI*